COLLEGE OF AEROSPACE DOCTRINE, RESEARCH AND EDUCATION

AIR UNIVERSITY

Understanding Islam and Its Impact on Latin America

CURTIS C. CONNELL
Lieutenant Colonel, USAF

CADRE Paper No. 21

Air University Press
Maxwell Air Force Base, Alabama 36112-6615

March 2005

Air University Library Cataloging Data

Connell, Curtis C.
    Understanding Islam and its impact on Latin America / Curtis C. Connell.
        p. ; cm. – (Cadre paper, 1537-3371 ; 21)
    Includes bibliographical references.

    1. Islamic fundamentalism. 2. Terrorism—Latin America. 3. Islam—Latin America. I. Title. II. Series. III. Air University (U.S.). College of Aerospace Doctrine, Research and Education.

    303.625/09/8—dc22

This CADRE Paper and others in the series are available electronically at the Air University Research Web site http://research.maxwell.af.mil and the AU Press Web site http://aupress.maxwell.af.mil.

CADRE Papers

CADRE Papers are occasional publications sponsored by the Airpower Research Institute of Air University's College of Aerospace Doctrine, Research and Education (CADRE). Dedicated to promoting the understanding of air and space power theory and application, these studies are published by Air University Press and broadly distributed to the US Air Force, the Department of Defense and other governmental organizations, leading scholars, selected institutions of higher learning, public-policy institutes, and the media.

All military members and civilian employees assigned to Air University are invited to contribute unclassified manuscripts that deal with air and/or space power history, theory, doctrine or strategy, or with joint or combined service matters bearing on the application of air and/or space power.

Authors should submit three copies of a double-spaced, typed manuscript and an electronic version of the manuscript on removable media along with a brief (200-word maximum) abstract. The electronic file should be compatible with Microsoft Windows and Microsoft Word—Air University Press uses Word as its standard word-processing program.

Please send inquiries or comments to
Chief of Research
Airpower Research Institute
CADRE
401 Chennault Circle
Maxwell AFB AL 36112-6428
Tel: (334) 953-5508
DSN 493-5508
Fax: (334) 953-6739
DSN 493-6739
E-mail: cadre.research@maxwell.af.mil

Contents

Foreword

Lt Col Curtis C. Connell hits a sensitive key in his observation that Islamic terrorism became one of the most important American security concerns after the attacks of 11 September 2001. Having spent three years as assistant air attaché in Buenos Aires, he sought to combine a fresh interest in Latin America with his desire to learn more about the nature of radical Islamic fundamentalism and its virulent association with terrorism. His fellowship year at Harvard University and guidance of his professors encouraged him to coalesce interests into a combined study of Islamic fundamentalism and its manifestation in Latin America. At the end of the term, he produced this very useful and attractive monograph, *Understanding Islam and Its Impact on Latin America.*

The initial question of this study concerns the debate between those who believe in a general Islamic threat, as defined most eloquently by Samuel P. Huntington in *The Clash of Civilizations and the Remaking of World Order,* and others who see a small band of religious fanatics who have hijacked Islam from the moderate majority. This question about the source of terrorism has importance to the major Islamic nations as it does for Latin American countries, where Muslims are a largely undistinguishable minority.

The preliminary answer for Latin America is that the United States should not be alarmed at the potential for Islamic fundamentalism, but sufficiently concerned to keep a watchful eye on future developments. In fact Connell suggests that the demographics do not favor the growth of an effective radical movement. If there are too few Muslims in Latin America to birth radicalism, there is on the other hand, a very active and extensive native, non-Islamic terrorism. The author connects these dots because he sees a latent connection to Muslims in the areas where terrorist organizations and drug traffickers proliferate. It is a potentially easy step for incipient Muslim radicals to get caught up and find beneficial purpose with these criminals. For example, the US dependence on imported petroleum and natural gas and a vulnerable transportation system provide an attractive target for Islamic terrorists, one they have used in the past.

Understanding Islam and Its Impact on Latin America was written as part of the Air Force Fellows research requirement. The College of Aerospace Doctrine, Research and Education (CADRE) is pleased to publish this study as a CADRE Paper and thereby make it available to a wider audience within the Air Force and beyond.

DANIEL R. MORTENSEN
Chief of Research
Airpower Research Institute, CADRE

About the Author

Lt Col Curtis C. Connell was commissioned in May 1983 as a Distinguished Graduate of the Air Force Officer Training School. His career includes a wide variety of operational assignments. Colonel Connell served as an instructor pilot in three diverse flying missions: T-37 instructor pilot, Laughlin AFB, TX; C-141 strategic airlift instructor pilot, McChord AFB, WA; and E-4B (Boeing 747) command and control chief evaluator pilot, Offutt AFB, NE. Additionally, he has served as commander, 1st Airborne Command Control Squadron (E-4B), Offutt AFB, and assistant air attaché at the US Embassy, Buenos Aires, Argentina. Selected as a 2004 National Defense Fellow, Colonel Connell completed studies at the John M. Olin Institute for Strategic Studies at Harvard University. He currently serves on the Air Staff as the chief, Asia/Pacific region, Air and Space Operations.

Colonel Connell earned his baccalaureate degree in Architectural Studies at the University of Nebraska, Lincoln, and is a Distinguished Graduate of Squadron Officer School, Maxwell AFB, AL. He earned the Master of Science degree in Aeronautical Science and Technology from Embry-Riddle Aeronautical University, Offutt AFB Extension Campus. He is a graduate of Air Command and Staff College, Maxwell AFB, and Armed Forces Staff College, Norfolk, VA. His major awards include the Defense Meritorious Service Medal, Meritorious Service Medal with two oak leaf clusters, Air Force Aerial Achievement Medal with one oak leaf cluster, and Air Force Commendation Medal. He is married to the former Cecilia Ruiz Calvillo of Guadalajara, Mexico. They have three children, Nina, Natalie, and Seth.

Acknowledgments

For my USAF Senior Developmental Education, I was blessed with a wonderful opportunity as a National Defense Fellow at the John M. Olin Institute for Strategic Studies, Harvard University. During the year, my interaction with numerous scholars knowledgeable on Islam and terrorism, attendance at lectures and debates on the topic, and time spent away from the "regular Air Force" to contemplate and think about the topic were invaluable.

Initially I was torn between a desire to focus my research solely on Latin America instead of radical Islam. My three-year assignment as the assistant air attaché in Buenos Aires had given me additional insights about the region that I desired to further develop. I thank Prof. Jorge Dominguez, the director of Harvard's Weatherhead Center for International Affairs, for suggesting a blending of the two topics, as well as Prof. Monica Duffy Toft, assistant director of the Olin Institute, for her encouragment. A special acknowledgment goes to Prof. Samuel Huntington, director of the Olin Institute, for his keen insights into culture and his course on religion and global politics.

Curtis C. Connell

Chapter 1

Introduction

Since 11 September 2001 (9/11)—that dreadful day forever etched in the memories of people around the world—Westerners have displayed increased interest, curiosity, and questioning of Islam. Numerous books, op-ed pieces, and scholarly research have addressed this subject. Many of these works try to explain why Islam—and, in particular, radical or fundamentalist Islam—is seen as a threat to Western security. Some scholars have suggested the basic problem is not terrorism but one of religion and ideology, at least as perceived by Islamic fundamentalists. Pres. George W. Bush said, "Our war is against evil, not against Islam.[1]" This is true. Unless Islamic extremists are convinced of this reality, the United States may underestimate the threat.

The first portion of this paper looks at various perspectives of "Islam" and the "Islamic threat." Is the Islamic threat simply a small band of religious fanatics who have hijacked Islam, or is it more on the grand scale of Samuel P. Huntington's *The Clash of Civilizations and the Remaking of World Order?*[2] Some scholars argue that promoting moderate Islam is the solution to countering the radical threat. The struggle within Islam between moderates and radicals has implications not only for Islamic countries, but also for regions where Muslims comprise a minority population, including Latin America and the Caribbean.

Whether US national security policy makers should be concerned about radical Islamic influence, support, and actions in pockets of Latin America and the Caribbean is an open question. Research suggests a mild concern regarding the level of Islamic fundamentalism in Latin America and the Caribbean, but no great cause for alarm and apprehension.

There are several keys to understanding why the Islamic threat in Latin America and the Caribbean is nominal. First and foremost, the demographics do not favor the growth of Islamic fundamentalism because not many Muslims live in the region.

Second, while the region has a rather extensive history of terrorist attacks, they have not come from Islamic groups. What exists in Latin America is a history of Islamic support activities, especially by Shiite groups such as Hezbollah, but not by radicals like al-Qaeda.

However, in certain areas within the region—for example Venezuela's Margarita Island and the Tri-Border Area (TBA) between Argentina, Brazil, and Paraguay—terrorist support activities probably necessitate extra vigilance. A nexus between terrorist organizations and criminal elements including drug traffickers is possible, but the lack of hard evidence makes that speculative.

Ignoring the possibility of an Islamic threat in Latin America is a mistake. The key to a successful national security policy is continuing US cooperation with Latin American partners through cooperative structures. Fortunately, organizations are in place to facilitate this course of action.

Notes

1. George W. Bush, remarks in the Oval Office, Washington, DC, 28 September 2001.

2. Samuel P. Huntington, *The Clash of Civilizations and the Remaking of World Order*, 1st ed. (New York: Simon and Schuster, 1997).

Chapter 2

Understanding "Islamic Fundamentalism"

As with many who write about controversial topics, the defenders of Islamic fundamentalism seek the high ground by defining the terms from their perspective. This chapter explores various scholarly and intellectual perspectives of Islam. This is a major undertaking due to the volume of resources published since 9/11. However, a concise consolidation of these myriad viewpoints should assist in understanding Islamic fundamentalism.

One of the first challenges when viewing Islam through Western eyes is the absence of an Arabic word for Islam as a religion. According to the Quran, Islam is *Deen*, and *Deen* is usually translated as religion or *mathhab*. However, *Deen* from the Muslims' perspective is not only a "religion," but also a code of life, a social system, an all-encompassing law and structure that comes from Allah alone. *Mathhab* means a passage or path made by man, which would apply to every other religion but Islam.[1] This is one of the first clues of a possible chasm between followers of Islam and those of Western democracy ideals.

Even scholars of Islam have a difficult time deciding what to call the various followers of Islam. The terms *political Islam, Islamism, traditional Islam, radical Islam, Wahhabism, Salafism, militant Islam, Islamic movement, and moderate Islam* are all pregnant with meaning.[2] The bias of each author becomes quite apparent when investigating the different scholarly perspectives. The important point is Islamic fundamentalism's proximity to the religious mainstream, in contrast to the distance of Islamic modernism, puts Muslims at ease with its message.[3]

Into which category would Osama bin Laden and al-Qaeda fit? Through Western eyes, these two would probably be identified with radical Islam, maybe even an extreme radical Islamic category. On the other hand, some in the Islamic world may view bin Laden and al-Qaeda as fighting for the purest form of Islam. This paper refers to Muslims who believe they are adhering to the closest form of Islam as taught by their founder Muhammad as Islamic fundamentalists.

Perspectives of Islam

Islam has a history full of conflict from the death of Muhammad in A.D. 632 to the present. Islam comprises two main divisions: the great majority are Sunnis and the minority, around 17 percent, are Shiites. Not only do followers of Shi'a Islam constitute a majority of the Muslims in Iran and Iraq, but these countries also have the largest concentration of Shiites in the world. Saudi Arabia has a majority of Sunnis that practice a stricter and more conservative form of Islam called Wahhabism. Sufis, or teachers and practitioners of spiritual Islam, are a large community within both Sunni and Shi'a Islam. There are also many sects within Sunni and Shi'a traditions.

Regardless of the various divisions, sects, and practices of Islam, two perspectives dominate Western scholarly circles today. In one camp, those that view the Islamic resurgence as a major concern to the West could be called confrontationalists. The other group could be called accommodationists and view Islam more as a religion of peace that is given a "bad image" by a small minority of radicals and terrorists. The accommodationists see the confrontationalists' stance as creating an imaginary united Islam, and argue the Arab/Islamic world is much more divided than some Western commentators would like to admit. Many fall in between these opposing sides. Here's a sampling of perspectives.

Confrontationalists

Some of the better known in this camp are Harvard University's Samuel Huntington, Princeton University's Bernard Lewis, and Daniel Pipes of the US Institute for Peace. The grand overarching viewpoint is characterized by Huntington's *Clash of Civilizations* concept and a resurgence of the Islamic ideals, politics, and culture.[4]

According to Huntington, Muslims are turning toward Islam as a source of identity, meaning, stability, legitimacy, development, power, and hope. He calls this an Islamic Resurgence since Muslims comprise one-fifth of the world's population and the movement has implications similar to other major movements like the Protestant Reformation and the revolutions in the

United States and Russia. The Islamic cultures are making renewed efforts to find solutions, not in Western ideologies, but in Islam. There is an acceptance of modernity but a rejection of Western culture. There is also a desire to use Islam as the guide to life in the modern world. Religion is seen as perhaps the central force that motivates and mobilizes Muslims.[5]

The extent of this movement is pervasive throughout the Muslim world. By the middle of the 1990s, every country with a predominantly Muslim population, except Iran, was more Islamic and Islamist culturally, socially, and politically than it had been 15 years earlier. The majority of Muslims see Islam as the solution to their development problems and resent Western influence in their culture. This Resurgence is an effort to modernize their countries, but in a distinctly Islamic manner. It is mainstream, not extremist; pervasive, not isolated; and a rededication to Islam by Muslim populations in the view of Huntington.[6]

Historian Bernard Lewis views the clash from the broad perspective of almost 1,400 years of Islamic history. His central theme is that from the seventh century until the Ottomans' failed second attempt to sack Christian Vienna in 1683, Muslims and their culture were dominant and powerful throughout the Islamic world. During the last three centuries, Islam has been on the defensive and Muslims have watched in horror and humiliation as the Christian civilizations of Europe and North America overshadowed them militarily, economically, and culturally.[7]

Lewis states, "In a sense, (Muslims) have been hating us for centuries, and it's very natural that they should. You have this millennial rivalry between two world religions, and now, from their point of view, the wrong one seems to be winning."[8] The notion of jihad is especially important in understanding this rivalry. Even though there is debate among Islamic scholars about the meaning of jihad, Lewis claims that for most of recorded Muslim history the correct interpretation is an armed struggle for the defense or advancement of Muslim power. Although primarily a fundamentalist idea, it is not that far out of the Islamic mainstream to consider this struggle continuing until the entire world either adopts Islam or submits to Muslim rule.[9]

5

Daniel Pipes describes the challenge in terms of Islamism, a terroristic and militant version of Islam with totalitarian roots in its struggle against moderate Islam. Even though he does not paint the picture as a pure "clash of civilizations," he believes the majority of Muslims support the ideology and beliefs of the fundamentalists. This helps explain the joy within the Muslim world following the attacks on 9/11.[10] Furthermore, the struggle between the West and the Islamic world is ultimately one of ideas and armies, not of law enforcement or religion. Just as World War II and the Cold War were ideological conflicts, Islamism has a grip on the majority of Muslims and this must be defeated. Pipes thinks militant Islam is the problem, but moderate Islam is the solution.[11]

Accommodationists

The Accommodationists view the Islamic world as very fragmented and divided from within, not as a unified block. This viewpoint claims the confrontationalists are creating a civilizational threat that comes from historical fallacy. These scholars tend to blame the radicalization of Muslims on US policies such as support for Israel, long-standing hegemony of the West, and support for oppressive and degenerate regimes in the Middle East. This camp attempts to understand and explain the reasons behind the fundamentalism of Islam and points out that radicalism flourishes where there is an absence of economic equality and political freedom. Some of the scholars associated with this position are Georgetown University's John Esposito, Columbia University's Edward Said (recently deceased), and Cato Institute's Leon Hadar.

Esposito posits the West's rising perception of "Islamic radicalism" may be more about filling the security threat vacuum left by the ending of the Cold War than a "clash of civilizations." He does not deny the growth of Islam and Islamic movements, but says it is simply wrong to tie the violent actions of a few with the broad and legitimate democratic aspirations of many. He stresses this phenomenon is more of an Islamic revivalism than resurgence. Revivalism in this sense is a return to Islam in personal and public life that will ensure the restoration of Islamic identity, values, and power, but still accept modernization.[12]

Esposito criticizes the sensationalized and monolithic approach of the confrontationalists that reinforces generalizations and stereotypes of Muslims. The focus on radicalism and equating Islam with extremism that threatens the West is too common in the media and government, he says. This selective analysis fails to tell the whole story of Islam and provide a full context for a wide variety of Muslim attitudes, events, and diversity. He thinks the vast majority of Muslims have little interest in the radical or fundamentalist movements. The concept that Islam and Muslims are portrayed as the instigators and protagonists in 14 centuries of warfare is wrongheaded.[13]

Contrary to conventional wisdom, the resurgence of Islam and modernization are compatible, Esposito argues. The Islamists desire to bring their societies up to technological levels of modern industrial society but within Islamic civil society and without Western influences.[14]

Edward Said is probably best known for his defense of the Palestinians and his criticism of how the West makes malicious generalizations about Islam based on Orientalism. According to Said, Orientalism occurs when the world is divided up into an "us versus them" mentality, viewing Islam as a threatening "other." The perception of the Islamic threat only exists because the West generally depicts Muslims as fanatical, violent, and irrational.[15] In other words, the West has an awareness problem and an incorrect understanding of Islam because of a desire to compartmentalize the world.

According to Leon Hadar, Islam is neither unified nor a threat to the West. The supposed worldwide threat from militant Islam has simply replaced the perception of danger experienced during the Cold War from Soviet communism. Instead of the Red Menace, the West has made the Green Peril, green being the color of Islam, our new global threat.[16] Islam is a religion, not a radical ideology threatening Western peace. He claims it is a mistake to portray the struggle between militant Islam and the West as a zero-sum game that can only end in the defeat of one or the other. This supposed monolithic threat is nothing more than taking isolated events and trends in the Muslim world and using the old Cold War jargon to describe the struggle with Islam.[17]

Islam is also open to various interpretations and is used to support democracy, dictatorship, republicanism, and monarchy. Islamic fundamentalism should not be viewed as a disease that spreads to infect whole populations. In fact, it is conceivable that a new Islamic force will play the same constructive political role that the Protestant reformation played in Europe.[18]

Islamic Anti-Western Rage: Historic and Strategic Explanations

Why do Islamic terrorists kill and what explains their anti-Western rage? Did Americans stir up the rage and bring it on themselves because of US policies? Maybe their rage is less a clash against the West than a conflict between Sunnis and Shiites. What if all Islamic fundamentalists' demands were met including resolving the Israeli-Palestinian conflict, no Western presence in the Islamic world, and Islamic rule in the region? Would there still be a threat?

The answers to these simple, but critical questions are as important as defining Islam. Later in this paper, the focus turns to Latin America to evaluate the threat from Islamic fundamentalism and Islamists. The answers may have policy implications for the region, either to discount the threat or raise a legitimate concern. But first, this section explores possible avenues to understanding the roots of Islamic fundamentalists' anger.

Impact of Colonialism

For nearly 1,000 years, the Islamic world enjoyed a position of power, influence, and prestige. Colonial expansion by European powers throughout the Middle East brought this era to a close. Not since the Crusades had the West and Muslims clashed over lands and influence in areas considered Islamic. The colonial period may have impacted Muslims more than any other peoples. First, Islamic civilization places heavy emphasis on control of the land, so the loss of sovereignty to the Europeans had a lasting effect. Second, Islamic autonomism provided Muslims with a unique drive to defy foreign domination. Unlike other peoples that were colonialized, the Muslims continued to resist. Because

Islam requires its adherents to wield political power, the colonial experience especially bruised Muslims.[19]

Today, Muslims are concerned about how to modernize and deal with globalization. They generally have an admiration for what the West does mixed with resentment that the United States and Europe fare so well. Muslims desire the achievements of the West but are unwilling to emulate its actions. There is an emotional rejection of the West, but at the same time a material dependence.[20]

United States Foreign Policy

Rather than focusing on religious and cultural differences as a cause of the hostility, a number of scholars place the source of Islamic militancy on US foreign policy. They argue that Muslim extremists like Osama bin Laden loathe the United States primarily because of its foreign policy. This judgment is largely based on recent public opinion polls taken in the Islamic world.

In early 2003, Zogby International conducted a survey involving 2,620 men and women in Egypt, Jordan, Lebanon, Morocco, and Saudi Arabia. Most reported "unfavorable attitudes" toward the United States and indicated their hostility was based more on US policy than their values. Not surprisingly, the issue that arouses the most hostility is the Israeli-Palestinian conflict and the Muslim perception of US-caused Palestinian suffering.[21]

Viewed from an exclusively Western perspective, the creation of the state of Israel represented Jewish national redemption, especially when considering the Holocaust and the centrality of Jewish presence in evangelical Christian thought about Palestine. But from an Islamic and Arab perspective, the state of Israel has never been seen this way. They view Zionism in Palestine as trampling the existing Arab majority, destroying Palestinian society, and dispossessing the Arab inhabitants. The dominant view in the Islamic world is that the pro-Israel lobby shapes American foreign policy regarding the Arab-Israeli conflict, which intensifies their anger at the United States.[22]

The Zogby poll also found that most Arabs have a different perspective of the US-led war in Iraq. A strong majority felt the United States attacked Iraq to gain control of Iraqi oil and to help

Israel. They do not accept the premise that the United States overthrew Saddam Hussein out of humanitarian motives.[23]

In fact, most Muslims view the US fight against terror as a war against the Islamic world. A 2003 Pew survey found that even Indonesians, Pakistanis, and Turks were either somewhat or very worried about a potential US threat to their countries. This is surprising because these are countries whose governments generally cooperate with the United States in the war on terror. It's more than startling that roughly half of the Muslims surveyed listed bin Laden as one of the three world figures in whom they had the most confidence "to do the right thing."[24]

Presence of Foreign Military Forces

Robert Pape from the University of Chicago posits a similar but more straightforward explanation for all terrorism, not just Islamic terrorism. He has compiled a database of every suicide bombing and attack around the globe from 1980 to 2001, a total of 188. He found that a Marxist-Leninist group called the Tamil Tigers in Sri Lanka committed the most of these attacks, 75 in all.

Pape's research suggests little connection between suicide terrorism and religion. Rather, what most suicide terrorist campaigns have in common is a specific secular and strategic goal. That primary goal in most cases is to coerce liberal democracies to withdraw military forces and control from territory that the terrorists consider their homeland. Although religion is often used as a tool by terrorist organizations in recruiting and other efforts, it is not their root cause. Lebanon, Israel, Sri Lanka, Kashmir, and Chechnya are each experiencing conflicts where suicide terrorists are striving to establish or maintain political self-determination by compelling a democratic power to withdraw.[25]

Globalization

If US foreign policy or the presence of military forces is a source of Muslims' anger, an even more encompassing root of anger may be globalization and the opposition to secular modern states. Viewed from the Islamic fundamentalist perspective, globalization represents secularism and a force in opposition to Islam. This conflict is not just a worldly struggle in their eyes, but also a sacred battle against the secular state represented by the United States.

Under the license of religion, fundamentalists wrap themselves in moral legitimacy and employ violence in assaulting symbols of global economic and political power. Religion has provided them a metaphor of cosmic war—a fight between good and bad, truth and evil. The attacks on the World Trade Center and the United Nations headquarters in Baghdad, symbols of globalization, were in that sense very religious.[26]

An important distinction must be made between different aspects of modernity and globalization. In one sense, the al-Qaeda network is a modern, transnational player, a symbol of globalization. Its members are sophisticated and technically skilled professionals, come from different nationalities, and use modern communications. In this sense, fundamentalists are not opposed to modernity and globalization, so long as it fits their own purposes. But they loath the Western-style modernity that they perceive secular globalization is forcing upon them.[27] This push/pull and a need to compromise to develop and modernize can be terribly frustrating to fundamentalists.

This resistance to Western-style modernity reminds some Muslims of prior colonialism. A leader in the Palestinian terrorist group Hamas gave his opinion about globalization in an interview. "Globalization is just a new colonial system. It is America's attempt to dominate the rest of the world economically rather than militarily. It will worsen the gap between rich and poor. America is trying to spread its consumer culture. These values are not good for human beings. The problem with pursuing capitalism as an end itself is that the name of the game is the dollar. In the West, money really does talk. This is bad for the human beings. It leads to disaster for communities."[28]

Islamic Angst: Psychological and Religious Struggles

Thus far, this paper has given some possible explanations for Islamists' rage and anger toward the West, focusing on strategic issues. However, it seems unlikely that colonialism, the Crusades, globalization, or military presence fully explain their loathing and hatred. There may be psychological, religious, or deeper spiritual issues that provide additional reasons. Also, the profound chasm between the Sunnis and the Shiites, or for that matter the clash between the moderates and fundamentalists, both need exploration. Perhaps the West is simply caught in the middle of rival factions vying for political power in the name of religion.

Although the Islamic rage seems to be a recent phenomenon, it could have deeper roots in history. Various explanations and perspectives follow to help explain Islamic angst and anguish.

Humiliation

Renowned terrorism expert Jessica Stern highlights one of the most basic psychological reasons for this rage in a recent book, *Terror in the Name of God*. Stern devotes an entire chapter to why she thinks humiliation is a major causal factor giving rise to desperation and uncontrollable rage among Palestinians. She discovered an epidemic of despair and individual hopelessness in interviews with Palestinians at many different levels of society, from professionals to terrorists. The Islamic terrorist leaders are able to tap into this sense of outrage and humiliation to encourage youth to murder Israeli civilians.[29]

One can argue that the despair and hopelessness are limited to Palestinians and caused by Israeli actions in the West Bank and Gaza or Israeli support in the West. However, because of the special role that Jerusalem plays in Islam, this sense of humiliation probably extends throughout the Islamic world. Granted, the Israeli-Palestinian conflict has its own set of dynamics, but it offers a possible explanation for the rage among many Muslims, not just Palestinians. Could this rage and/or desire for violent action extend back even further?

The Assassins

An early sect of Shi'a Islam, called the Ismailis, began a practice that may have laid some early groundwork for today's Islamic terrorists, especially those that target fellow Muslims.

Beginning in the medieval period and within a few centuries after the founding of Islam, this secretive sect was known for unprecedented employment of planned, systematic, and long-term use of terror as a political weapon. While not the first group in history to use murder to accomplish political goals, the Ismailis, unlike previous political murderers, used terror for strategic effects.[30]

In fact, the English word *assassin* has its roots in the Arabic language. During the Crusades, the Christian warriors were warned about the Assassins and the precautions needed to guard against them. Although the exact origin of the Assassins was not known, the Crusaders regarded them as hired killers who were ruthless and competent.[31]

The vast majority of victims, however, were Muslims, not Crusaders. The Assassins' attacks were directed not against outsiders, but against the dominant elite and the prevailing ideas in the Islamic world of their time. Unlike today's Islamic terrorists, the Assassins never harmed ordinary people, but focused on the great and powerful.[32]

Several parallels from the Assassins apply today. After they struck a victim, there was no attempt at escape or rescue. On the contrary, to survive a mission was seen as a disgrace. This was not considered suicide, which has always been forbidden in Islam. Another constant theme of the Assassins was to purify the faith and overthrow the existing Sunni order in Islam to replace it with their own. This theme of striving to purify the faith may still be a factor today.

Impact of Wahhabism

Less than a century had passed after the death of the founder of Islam before major conflict arose among Muslims. The struggle for the heart of Islam that began in the seventh century between Sunnis and Shiites continues today. Some scholars suggest Western political and intellectual leaders fail to adequately understand the internal crisis in Islam and the conflict between tradition and extremism. Author Stephen Schwartz has argued in his book, *The Two Faces of Islam*, that the primary root of these problems is Wahhabism.

Wahhabism is the puritanical form of Islam founded by Muhammad ibn Abdul-Wahhab in the early eighteenth century. Ibn Abdul-Wahhab called for a return to tradition and what he proclaimed was the purest form of Islam. Ibn Abdul-Wahhab's goal was for all Muslims to surrender to his vision of an original, authentic Islam such as he imagined had existed in the time of Muhammad. He successfully converted the Bedouins living in the deserts of Saudi Arabia, including Muhammad Ibn Saud, the forerunner of the House of Saud. Ibn Abdul-Wahhab and Saud agreed to coordinate to expand their influence and power. Saud would be the political leader, or emir, and Ibn Abdul-Wahhab would be the religious leader, the sheik.[33] So began one of the most influential movements that is impacting Islamic fundamentalism today.

From its beginning, Wahhabism declared the entirety of existing Islam to be unbelief, and traditional Muslims to be unbelievers subject to robbery, murder, and sexual violation. They viewed Shiite Muslims genocidally, as non-Muslims worthy of annihilation. According to Schwartz, this fundamentalist form of Islam attacked the traditional, spiritual Islam or Sufism that dominates in the Balkans, Turkey, Central Asia, India, Malaysia, and Indonesia. Additionally, Wahhabism has spawned so-called neo-Wahhabist movements such as the Egyptian Muslim Brotherhood, Pakistani Islamists, and Palestinian Hamas movement in Israel. Schwartz claims the majority of Islamic extremist violence in the world today can be attributed to Wahhabist-inspired groups like al-Qaeda or other terrorist movements that embrace this distinct ultra-radical form of Islamism.[34]

While Islamic scholars debate the exact definition of Wahhabism, there is little question that Saudi Arabia embraces this form of Islam. The supposed goal of the Wahhabi-Saudi alliance is to tear down the traditional Islam present from Bosnia-Herzegovina to South Africa and from Morocco to the Philippines, and to replace it with their extremist, ultrarigid, and puritanical version of Islam. They attempt this through indoctrination, infiltration, and financial subsidies from Saudi supporters. In addition to the main aim of capturing and guiding the global Islamic community, Wahhabism doctrines are deeply suffused with hatred of the other religions.[35] If Wahhabism is indeed the penetrating dogma behind much of the radical and fundamentalist Islam, is the Saudi state a collaborator and sponsor of terrorists?

Battle for Heart of Islam in Saudi Arabia

Whether or not the Saudi state is a willing or unwilling sponsor of Wahhabi-inspired Islamic radicals may depend on who is indeed ruling the roost. One very probable explanation is the struggle for influence and power between two ruling factions or fiefdoms in the royal family. Since King Fahd's stroke in 1995, the unanswered question of succession has remained. On one hand, Crown Prince Abdullah is the de facto head of the monarchy, but his power is not solidified. His half-brother and interior minister, Prince Nayef, controls the secret police and casts a longer and darker shadow.[36]

The struggle for the heart of Islam in Saudi Arabia, and in effect the worldwide majority Sunni Muslims, may come down to which prince has the most influence. Abdullah is a moderate, a supporter of liberal political and economic reforms. He adheres to the Islamic doctrine of *Taqarub*. This doctrine supports rapprochement between Muslims and non-Muslims as well as peaceful coexistence with nonbelievers. Nayef, on the other hand, is a conservative who sides with the Wahhabi clerics and takes directions from an anti-American religious establishment that shares many goals with al-Qaeda. Nayef supports the Islamic doctrine of *Tawhid*, or monotheism as defined by Ibn Abdul-Wahhab. For the most radical clerics, this doctrine promotes a puritanical form of Islam whose enemies include Christians, Jews, Shiites, and moderate Sunni Muslims. This doctrine translates into a foreign policy that supports jihad and worldwide funding for Wahhabism.[37]

One should not underestimate the Wahhabi radicals' hatred and fear of Shiites. As much as the radicals dislike Abdullah's moderate sentiments, they may be willing to accept his control of Saudi Arabia as long as the Wahhabi clerics do not perceive a political compromise with Shiites. The Shiites offer an alternative notion of Islamic community and history as well as political interests that coincide with those of Sunni reformers. The Wahhabis' worst nightmare is formation of a powerful political bloc

15

between moderate reformers throughout the Islamic world, both Sunni and Shiite.[38]

The winds of moderate reform in the Islamic world, whether with democratic overtones or simply traditional Islamic theology, are of great concern to fundamentalists inside and outside of Saudi Arabia. This struggle for the soul of Islam could have implications for all regions of the world, including Latin America and the Caribbean.

Clash or Collusion of Islamic Fundamentalists?

It is difficult to develop a concise and comprehensive perspective of Islam, or even Islamic fundamentalism in a brief paper. It does not take long to discover the wide variety of explanations and opinions of this religion. Often, as more "layers of the onion" are uncovered, Islamic fundamentalism becomes even more perplexing and confusing.

Several broad conclusions can be drawn about Islam. First, there is a general tendency for the vast majority of Muslims to tightly fuse politics and religion, whether traditional or fundamentalist, Sunni or Shiite. Second, Islamic followers are generally of two types: devout, fundamentalist Muslims who adhere to the letter of the law or what they think is the letter of the law, and moderates who are Muslim by birth, culture, or tradition. What makes these moderates unique is a tendency to either implicitly or tacitly support the actions of the fundamentalists. It's unusual to hear Islamic moderates condemn fundamentalists' actions. Third, what separates Islamic fundamentalists from other religious fundamentalists and makes them inherently more threatening to US national security is their belief in violence to proliferate, enforce, and spread Islam. Finally, this devout core of believers may not be peripheral, although they probably represent only a small minority of the more than one billion Muslims in the world.

As was clearly displayed on 9/11, the struggle occurring in the Islamic world does have implications for the rest of the world. The following chapter explores whether Islamic fundamentalism is having an impact on Latin America and if there is a connection to the turmoil in the Islamic world.

Notes

1. Mohammed Abdul Malek, "A Knowledge of Arabic and Its Importance," *A Study of the Quran, Universal Guidance for Mankind,* January 2000, http://members.aol.com/Mamalek2/qbook2.htm.

2. Haneef James Oliver, "What is a Salafi and What is Salafism?" *The Wahhabi Myth,* May 2003, http://thewahhabimyth.com. According to author, Salafis are true followers of the Prophet Muhammad who is also called Salaf.

3. Milton Viorst, *In the Shadow of the Prophet, The Struggle for the Soul of Islam* (New York: Anchor Books, Doubleday, 1998), 19–20.

4. Samuel P. Huntington, *The Clash of Civilizations and the Remaking of World Order,* 1st ed. (New York: Simon and Schuster, 1997), 109–111.

5. Ibid., 109, 110.

6. Ibid., 110.

7. Peter Waldman, "Containing Jihad: A Historian's Take On Islam Steers US In Terrorism Fight—Bernard Lewis's Blueprint—Sowing Arab Democracy—Is Facing A Test in Iraq—The "Clash of Civilizations," *Wall Street Journal,* 3 February 2004, 1.

8. Ibid., 1.

9. Bernard Lewis, *The Crisis of Islam* (New York: Random House, 2003), 31–32.

10. Daniel Pipes, *Miniatures, Views of Islamic and Middle Eastern Politics* (London: Transaction Publishers, 2004), 2–3.

11. Daniel Pipes and Graham Fuller, "Combating the Ideology of Radical Islam," *Anglican Media Sydney,* 14 April 2003, http://www.anglicanmedia.com.au.news.archives/000961.php.

12. John L. Esposito, *The Islamic Threat, Myth or Reality?* 3d ed. (New York: Oxford University Press, 1999), 16–17.

13. Ibid., 218–220.

14. John L. Esposito and Francois Burgat, *Modernizing Islam* (London: Hurst & Company, 2003), 3–6.

15. David Barsamian, "Edward W. Said," *The Progressive,* November 2001, http://www.progressive.org/0901/intv1101.html.

16. Leon T. Hadar, "What Green Peril?" *Foreign Affairs,* Spring 1993, http://www.foreignaffairs.org/19930301faessay5172/leon-t-hadar/what-green-peril.html.

17. Leon T. Hadar, "The Green Peril: Creating the Islamic Fundamentalist Threat," *Policy Analysis,* CATO Institute, August 1992, 2–3.

18. Ibid., 35.

19. Daniel Pipes, *In the Path of God, Islam and Political Power* (New York: Basic Books, Inc., 1983), 188–190.

20. Ibid., 196–197.

21. Henry Munson, "Lifting the Veil," *Harvard International Review* 25, no. 4 (Winter 2004): 20.

22. Ussama Makdisi, "Anti-Americanism in the Arab World: An Interpretation of a Brief History," *The Journal of American History* 89, no. 2 (Septem-

ber 2002), http://www.historycooperative.org/journals/jah/89.2/makdisi. html.

23. Ibid., 22.

24. Ibid.

25. Robert Pape, "Dying to Kill Us," *New York Times*, 22 September 2003.

26. Mark Juergensmeyer, "Holy Orders, Religious Opposition to Modern States," *Harvard International Review* 25, no. 4 (Winter 2004): 34–35.

27. Ibid., 36.

28. Jessica Stern, *Terror in the Name of God, Why Religious Militants Kill* (New York: HarperCollins, 2003), 40–41.

29. Ibid., 32–62.

30. Bernard Lewis, *The Assassins, A Radical Sect in Islam* (New York: Basic Books, Inc, 2003), 129–130.

31. Ibid., 1–19.

32. Ibid., *xi.*

33. Ibid., 67–68.

34. Stephen Schwartz, *The Two Faces of Islam, The House of Saud from Tradition to Terror* (New York: Doubleday, 2002), 66–125.

35. Stephen Schwartz, "Defeating Wahabbism," *FrontPage Magazine*, October 2002, http://www.frontpagemag.com/Articles/ReadArticle.asp?ID=4178.

36. Michael Scott Doran, "The Saudi Paradox," *Foreign Affairs*, January/February 2004, 35–36.

37. Ibid., 36–39.

38. Ibid., 42–49.

Chapter 3

Islamic Fundamentalism in Latin America and the Caribbean

Islamic fundamentalism and terrorist activity in Latin America—whether the unsolved 1992 bombing of the Israeli Embassy in Buenos Aires or fundraising in the "Wild West" Tri-Border Area (TBA) between Argentina, Brazil, and Paraguay—does have a connection to events in the Middle East. This terrorist activity was part, and remains a part, of the global collision between those who uphold Western ideals and Islamic fundamentalists who do not hold a democratic worldview. Because of this nexus, discovering who or what is driving the Islamic fundamentalist "train" in Latin America and the Caribbean is significant. Is it the Iranian/Syrian/Lebanese-inspired Hezbollah Shiites, the Sunni/Wahabbi-motivated al-Qaeda, or somebody else? Furthermore, these terrorist groups may now be collaborating and morphing into new types of terrorist organizations.

Latin America is generally misunderstood by North Americans and is much more diverse than most realize. Even the topic of Islamic fundamentalism in Latin America draws skepticism.

Latin America and the Caribbean are home to almost 500 million inhabitants, who show startling contrasts between rich and poor, learned and illiterate, and democracy and dictatorship. It is a mistake to assume that everyone speaks Spanish and attends Catholic Mass. Granted, most inhabitants of the region are Catholic and are either of indigenous or Latin background (Spanish, Italian, or Portuguese).[1] But, as in the United States, virtually every ethnic background in the world is represented. These groups may include anyone from descendents of Africans brought to Latin America for slavery to Syrian and Lebanese immigrants.

In these small pockets of Arab, Indian, and African immigrants, Islam has gained a small footprint in Latin America and the Caribbean. Former Argentine President Carlos Menem is a significant example of how someone from one of these minorities can gain prominence. Born in Argentina of Syrian Muslim parents, he converted to Catholicism in order to become president in 1989.[2]

Muslim Demographics in the Region

Muslims probably represent less than one percent of the total population of South America. Even the most optimistic projection from Islamic sources is six million or less. One source notes the number of Islamic followers in Brazil at 1.5 million (less than one percent of the population) and in Argentina, 700,000 (two percent of the population).[3]

Another Islamic source indicates an even smaller percentage in Brazil—around one million, including 10,000 converts to Islam.[4] This low number of Islamic converts versus Muslims by ethnicity or birth could indicate a very tight or closed Islamic community in Brazil. More likely, Islam simply does not have much appeal for native Brazilians.

The majority of Muslims in Brazil are Syrian and Lebanese immigrants and their descendants. Some 11 million Syrian and Lebanese immigrants live throughout Brazil. Just over 10 percent consider themselves Muslim, while the vast majority claims the Catholic faith.[5]

Argentina has one of the most active Islamic groups in the region, called Islamic Organization of Latin America (IOLA). This is due to the slightly higher percentage of Muslims in Argentina as well as having the largest mosque in the region. The King Fahd Islamic Cultural Center in Buenos Aires is a $22 million structure completed in 2000 and inaugurated with Saudi Arabia's Crown Prince Abdullah in attendance. The center sits on 7.5 acres of prime real estate, valued at between $20 and $40 million, which was donated by Menem during his presidency. The 390,000-square-foot building has an auditorium, a primary and secondary school, dormitories, and underground parking.[6]

IOLA holds events to promote the unification of Muslims living in the region as well as the propagation of Islam. In March of 2003, IOLA sent 13 young Muslims from Argentina, Chile, Brazil, Uruguay, Bolivia, Paraguay, Venezuela, Curacao, Guatemala, Costa Rica, and Ecuador to Hajj.[7] This range of countries indicates the wide distribution of Muslims in Latin America and the Caribbean.

These small groups of Muslims scattered throughout the region surprise even experienced diplomats knowledgeable on Latin America. A 35-year veteran US diplomat who visited a small town in the southern Brazilian state of Parana shortly after the death of Iranian Shiite leader Ayatollah Khomeini in 1989 recalls his surprise at finding three mosques filled with Muslim Arabs mourning the death of Khomeini.[8]

Muslim demographics in the Caribbean area are similar to Latin America at around one percent of the total population, or 300,000, but with two notable exceptions in the English- and Dutch-speaking communities. The highest percentage of Muslims in the entire region exists in Dutch Suriname at just over 28 percent of its 425,000 inhabitants.[9] These Muslims are primarily Javanese from Indonesia, Indo-Pakistanis whose ancestors came as indentured laborers more than a century ago, and the Afro-Surinamese. The 140,000 English-speaking Muslims are evenly divided between Guyana (70,000 representing 10 percent of population), and Trinidad and Tobago (70,000 or six percent of population).[10]

The only two members of the Organization of Islamic Conference (OIC) in the Western hemisphere are Guyana (1998) and Suriname (1996). The Arab Islamic influence in both countries has grown since they joined the OIC. Because their tradition and ethnic backgrounds are rooted primarily in Java and Indo-Pakistan, they generally do not speak Arabic in the mosques and some of their practices could be considered unorthodox. Therefore, some Guyanese Muslims have trained in Saudi Arabia with the intent of "purifying" Islamic practices in Guyana.[11]

Islamic Terrorist Attacks in the Region

The demographics in Latin America and the Caribbean give little indication of Islamic fundamentalism or terrorism in the region. While Guyana and Suriname are recent members of the OIC, these two countries have no history of violent Islamic activity and only a minimal connection to Islamic fundamentalism.

Except for Guyana, Suriname, and Trinidad and Tobago, the extremely low percentage of Muslims in any country in the region hardly raises an eyebrow.

Looking into these pockets of Islamic followers, is there a history of terrorism or radicalism that provides clues to future activity? Latin American history is filled with examples of terrorism from revolutionary organizations such as Peru's *Sendero Luminoso* ("Shining Path") and Colombia's FARC, but these movements are not Islamic. Nevertheless, there are relevant examples in the region.

Trinidad and Tobago

In July 1990, Yasin Abu Bakr led a coup attempt by the black radical Muslim organization Jamaat al Muslimeen in Port-of-Spain, Trinidad. He and 114 rebels set off a car bomb that gutted the police station in front of the Parliament and then stormed into the legislature, spraying bullets, to gain control. The rebels took over the television station to announce they had seized control of the country. A six-day hostage crisis ensued while the rebels held Prime Minister Robinson and his cabinet. Twenty-five people were killed during the crisis. The rebels surrendered after a negotiated settlement with the government facilitated by US and UK ambassadors and Caribbean Community (CARICOM).[12]

Ironically, the coup attempt was triggered by the denial of a building permit for a mosque. Discontent in the black Islamic community had been brewing for more than 20 years due to struggles over government policies. After the failed coup attempt, the government razed Jamaat's compound consisting of a school and medical clinic. Ten years later the government made its first payment of $195,000 to Jamaat's members for damage incurred to their compound. This followed a $2.3 million fine levied on 58 Muslim radicals by Trinidad's high court for the bombing of the police headquarters.[13]

Buenos Aires

The 1992 suicide bombing of the Israeli Embassy in Buenos Aires is arguably the first Islamic terrorist attack in South America. Although the attack has yet to be officially solved, the bulk of the evidence points to the Iranian-backed Lebanese terrorist organization Hezbollah. A car, driven by a suicide bomber and loaded with explosives, smashed into the front of the embassy and detonated. The attack wounded 242 people and killed 29 Israelis and Argentine civilians. The probable motive for the attack came one month earlier when Israeli gunships attacked a motorcade in southern Lebanon, killing Sheik Abbas al-Musawi, leader of the Hezbollah terrorist group.[14]

While investigation of the embassy bombing dragged on for more than two years in the Argentine Supreme Court, an even more devastating terrorist bombing struck Buenos Aires' large Jewish community. The bombing of the Argentina Jewish Mutual Aid Association (AMIA) resulted in 87 deaths and more than 100 injuries.[15]

Although there have been several breakthroughs in the bombing investigations, both cases remain open. Despite repeated denials by the governments of Iran and Argentina, several important pieces of evidence point to their possible involvement or at least a desire to leave the cases unsolved. A 1998 telephone call intercepted from the Iranian Embassy in Argentina demonstrated Iran's involvement in the attack on the Israeli Embassy and led to expulsion of six of the seven Iranian diplomats.[16]

Failure to solve the cases may also be due in part to the involvement of former President Menem. According to the *New York Times,* which obtained a 100-page Argentine secret deposition, the Iranian government paid Menem $10 million to cover up the crime.[17] Regardless of who committed the bombings or who is responsible for delaying justice, the dynamic combination of Menem's Islamic heritage, the large Jewish population in Buenos Aires, and the quick retribution of Hezbollah indicate an environment ripe for Islamic terrorism and/or support.

Islamic Terrorist Support in the Region

The two bombings in Buenos Aires, most likely committed by Hezbollah, and the attempted coup in Trinidad by Jamaat al Muslimeen —all occurring more than 10 years ago—hardly constitute a profound and deep history of Islamic terrorism in

Latin America and the Caribbean. Although Latin American countries have struggled with domestic terrorism for decades, Islamic terrorist attacks do not seem to register high on their anxiety scale.

Should US policy makers, nevertheless, be concerned about Islamic fundamentalists activities in the region? While no bombings attributable to Islamic fundamentalists have occurred since 1994, there is a more recent history of Islamic fundamentalist support activities. The two geographic areas of primary concern are Venezuela's Margarita Island and the TBA between Argentina, Paraguay, and Brazil.

Tri-Border Area

The TBA has a somewhat "Wild West" reputation and lax rule of law, even by Latin American standards, especially in the Paraguayan sector. A large Arab community of roughly 30,000 primarily Lebanese and Syrian immigrants is involved in business enterprises there, both legal and illegal. Hezbollah and Hamas have a history stretching back a couple of decades of using the TBA for fundraising and other support. Although the area had been monitored for some time, the 1992 bombing in Buenos Aires increased scrutiny there. The attacks on 9/11 greatly intensified that attention.[18]

The area has been and remains a haven for illicit activities by organized crime and, most likely, terrorist groups. These groups use the TBA for smuggling, money laundering, product piracy, and drug and arms trafficking. The geography, social climate, economy, and permissive political environment allow criminals and corrupt officials to thrive by exchanging bribes or payoffs. It is difficult to determine whether these activities are crime- and/or terrorism-related. Numerous organized crime groups, including the Lebanese and Chinese Mafias, are known to use the TBA for illicit activities. The level of financial "transactions" is staggering. For example, the Paraguayan city of Cuidad del Este generated $12 to $13 billion in cash transactions annually as of 2001, making it the third largest money-handler worldwide behind Hong Kong and Miami. This figure may be declining due to closer Argentine and Brazilian customs controls.[19]

It is unknown exactly what portion of this illicit activity is committed by Islamic fundamentalists or terrorist groups. According to recent and extensive Library of Congress Federal Research Reports on the TBA, various Islamic terrorist groups have used the area for fundraising, drug trafficking, money laundering, plotting, and other activities in support of their organizations. From 1999 to 2001, Islamic extremist groups, specifically Hezbollah and Hamas, received up to $500 million from Arab residents on the Brazilian side of the border through Paraguayan financial institutions.[20]

Other Islamic terrorists groups thought to have a presence include Egypt's Al-Gama'a al-Islamiyya, Al-Jihad (Islamic Jihad), al-Qaeda, and al-Muqawamah, which is a pro-Iranian wing of the Lebanon-based Hezbollah. The large Arab community in the TBA also makes it highly conducive to establishment of sleeper cells. Although the TBA has one of the largest concentrations of Islamic extremists in Latin America, as many as 11,000 may have moved since late 2001 to other less closely watched Arab population centers in South America.[21] The bottom line is the TBA remains a fertile ground for illegal and unlawful behavior, but probably not quite to the extent of pre-9/11.

Margarita Island

Small groups of Muslims may be conducting similar support activities in other areas of Latin America. Research suggests that where pockets of Arab immigrants and/or followers of Islam exist, there is a potential for illicit support activity. One such example is a resort island off the coast of Venezuela and home to around 4,000 Arab immigrants, primarily Palestinians, Syrians, and Lebanese. Although this is a small percentage of Margarita Island's 300,000 residents and an even smaller percentage of the estimated 600,000 Venezuelan citizens of Arab descent, there are strong indications of support activities for Islamic terrorists.[22]

Although they comprise a small fraction of the island's population, the Arabs exert a disproportionate influence on daily life through their economic clout. The local cable television outlet carries al-Jazeera as well as channels from Lebanon and Syria. Women in headscarves work cash regis-

25

ters, and verses of the Quran are displayed on most shop counters. The Arabs are involved in retail businesses as well as travel agencies and banks. The Venezuelan government is aware of the Arab presence on the island and is investigating various allegations, but has found no terrorism links.[23]

Venezuela's ambassador to the United States denied accusations that the Chavez government has supported international terrorism in an address last October at the Center for Latin American Studies at the University of California-Berkeley. The ambassador dismissed out of hand accusations that Venezuela provided training for al-Qaeda terrorists on Margarita Island.[24]

Nevertheless, Gen James Hill, then commander of US Southern Command, specifically cited the existence of Islamic terrorist support activities in the TBA and Margarita Island in a 2003 speech. He elaborated on a connection between narco-traffickers and Islamic terrorists who generate funds by money laundering, document forgery, and arms trafficking. In the words of the general, "Simply put, direct drug sales and money laundering fund worldwide terrorists operations. That is fact, not speculation."[25]

Muslims' Geographic Connection with Terrorism

Although difficult to prove with certainty, the persistent connections between Muslims in Latin America and the presence of Islamic terrorism or support suggest a pattern. This blueprint indicates that if Islamic terrorists desire to use a region for safe haven purposes, illicit fundraising, money laundering, and so forth, they will congregate with or near followers of Islam. This is neither a startling discovery nor a profound concept; it simply follows what Islamic terrorists do in other areas of the world with Islamic populations. What makes Latin America and the Caribbean unique are a number of factors.

Islamic terrorism and support in this region are exceptional due to the demographics, geography, and lax rule of law. With few exceptions, each country in the region has an extremely high percentage of Catholics and very low percentage of Muslims. Even the vast majority of Arab immigrants are not Muslims, but Lebanese and Syrian Catholics. This Muslim minority tends to collect in pockets, whether in the TBA, Margarita Island, or Buenos Aires. More noteworthy, these pockets of Muslims tend to be either Lebanese or Syrian immigrants and followers of Shi'ism, not Sunni Islam or Wahabbism. The major exceptions are in Guyana, Suriname, and Trinidad and Tobago with their Javanese, Indo-Pakistani, or African heritage. They are not Shiites, but neither are they devout followers of Sunni Islam or Wahabbism despite attempts to "purify" their doctrine.

The historical evidence of Islamic terrorist events over the past couple of decades confirms this pattern. Although unresolved, the two Islamic terrorist bombings in Buenos Aires point to Hezbollah presence and support in Argentina. The attempted coup in Trinidad and Tobago is attributed to the black Islamic group Jamaat-al-Muslimeen. Although Sunni followers of Islam make up the majority of Muslims in the world, this is not true of Latin American demographics.

The wide-open geography and lax rule of law in Latin America also create a different dynamic from other areas of the world. Much of Latin America developed around urban centers that have grown into sprawling metropolitan areas like Buenos Aires or Sao Paulo. At the same time, there are large sections of undeveloped, unpopulated, and ungoverned areas that are vulnerable to misuse and illicit activities. Both of these geographic phenomena give rise to exploitation by all types of criminals and terrorists. General Hill summed up his view about the region's susceptibility:

> Today's foe is the terrorist, the narco-trafficker, the arms trafficker, the document forger, the international crime boss, and the money launderer. This threat is a weed that is planted, grown, and nurtured in the fertile ground of ungoverned spaces such as coastlines, rivers, and unpopulated border areas. This threat is watered and fertilized with money from drugs, illegal arms sales, and human trafficking. This threat respects neither geographical nor moral boundaries.[26]

This does not mean there is a clear nexus or connection between Islamic terrorists and narco-terrorists. It does mean the region has the right ingredients to foster the kind of support environment sought by Islamic terrorists. Even though places like the TBA appear a tangled web of organized crime groups and Islamic terrorists, General Hill does not believe there is cooperation and collaboration between the two.[27]

Notes

1. Thomas E. Skidmore and Peter H. Smith, *Modern Latin America* (New York: Oxford University Press, 2001), 2–5.

2. *Encyclopedia Wikipedia*, 2003 ed., "Carlos Saul Menem," 20 February 2004, http://en.wikipedia.org/wiki/Carlos_Saul_Menem.

3. Sr. N. Ballivan, "Country Perspectives, Latin America, The Spanish Ummah of the Muslim World," 12 December 2003, http://www.islamic-paths.org/Home/English/Countries/Latin_America/.

4. "Islam in Latin America: 'Lack of Islamic Literature in Brazil,'" *Latin American Muslim Unity*, 21 May 2001, http://www.latinmuslims.com/history/brazil_2000.html.

5. Mario Osava, "LATAM-US: Xenophobic Threats Target Arabs Everywhere," *World News, Inter Press Service*, 14 September 2001, http://www.oneworld.org/ips2/sept01/02_36_009.html.

6. Robert Elliot and Gilbert Le Grass, "Buenos Aires Gets Biggest Mosque in Latin America," *Daily News Yahoo.com*, 15 December 2003, http://daily news.yahoo.com/h/nm/20000925/wl/argentina_mosque_dc_1.html.

7. Sr. N. Ballivan.

8. Timothy Pratt, "US Eyes Jungle as Terror Threat Grows," *Sunday Herald Online*, 5 January 2003, http://www.sundayherald.com/30415.

9. "Muslim Situation in the Caribbean," *Muslim World League Journal*, 30 October 2003, http://www.geocities.com/.

10. Central Intelligence Agency, *The World Factbook*, 2003, 30 October 2003, http://www.cia.gov/cia/publications/factbook.

11. Raymond Chickrie, "Muslims in Guyana," *Muslims in Guyana: History, Traditions, Conflict and Change*, December 1999, 30 October 2003, http://www.WestHollywood/Park/6443/.

12. Winston Dookeran, deputy prime minister of Trinidad and Tobago, interviewed by author, 20 November 2003.

13. Angela Potter, "Muslims That Lead Failed Coup Fined," Associated Press, 16 January 2000, http://www.hvk.org/articles/0101/86.html.

14. *Encyclopedia Wikipedia*, 2003 ed. "Israeli Embassy Attack in Buenos Aires," 24 February 2004, http://en.wikipedia.org/wiki/Israeli_Embassy_Attack_in_Buenos_Aires.

15. *Jewish Virtual Library*, 2003 ed., "Terrorist Bombings in Argentina," 24 February 2004 http://www.us-israel.org/jsource/Terrorism/.

16. Ibid.

17. Larry Rohter, "Bomb Case Witness: Iran Paid Off Menem," *New York Times Service*, 22 July 2002, http://www.ourjerusalem.com/history/story/history20020724.html.

18. "Patterns of Global Terrorism-2001, Latin American Overview," US Department of State, Office of the Coordinator for Counterterrorism, 21 May 2001, http://www.state.gov/s/ct/pgtrpt/2001.html.

19. "Terrorist and Organized Crime Groups in the Tri-Border Area (TBA) of South America," The Library of Congress, Federal Research Division, July 2003, 2–4.

20. Ibid., 1, 27–28.

21. Ibid., 1–2.

22. Linda Robinson, "Terror Close to Home," *U.S. News & World Report* 135, no. 11 (6 October 2003): 20.

23. Scott Wilson, "U.S. probes Arabs on Venezuelan isle," *Washington Post,* 23 April 2002.

24. Jason Seawright, "The Official Perspective on Venezuelan Democracy," remarks at Center for Latin American Studies, UC-Berkeley, 30 October 2003, http://www.socrates.berkeley.edu:7001/Events/.

25. James Hill, "Building Security Cooperation in the Western Hemisphere," remarks at North-South Center, 3 March 2003, http://www.iwar.org.uk/news-achieve/2003/03-12/htm.

26. Ibid.

27. Gen James Hill, author's notes, question and answer forum, Massachusetts Institute of Technology faculty club, 26 February 2004.

Chapter 4

Today's Islamic Threat

Arguably, the US security policy establishment is more focused on Islamic fundamentalist terrorism than simply "terrorism." Furthermore, most of this interest is concentrated on Iraq and Afghanistan. The struggle occurring in the Islamic world between fundamentalists and moderates is of utmost importance not only to the future of the Middle East, but to other regions of the world as well.

Although Shiite fundamentalists such as Hezbollah certainly remain a threat, especially to Israel, it's the Sunni Wahabbi-fueled fundamentalists like al-Qaeda who pose the greater threat to US national security interests.

What, Who, and Where is the Islamic Terrorist Threat?

Fortunately, there does not appear to be a large presence of Wahabbi Islamic fundamentalists in Latin America and the Caribbean. That could mean the security concerns for the region are less than initially thought. Nevertheless, one cannot discount the role of Hezbollah Shiites, ad hoc Islamic fundamentalist groups, or possible connections between Wahabbis, Hezbollah, and/or drug traffickers.

Except in Guyana, Surinam, and Trinidad, the Muslim demographics of Latin America point to a preponderance of Lebanese and Syrian Shiites, not Sunnis. Are there Shiite fundamentalists embedded in these pockets of Islamic followers who are cooperating with al-Qaeda or other branches of radical Sunni Wahabbis?

Hezbollah-al-Qaeda Connection?

According to former CIA director George Tenet, such an alliance could be occurring in lawless regions like the TBA and Margarita Island. He cited an increase in low-level cooperation between al-Qaeda and Hezbollah and confirms that a "mixing and matching of capabilities, swapping of training, and the use of common facilities" could be happening.[1]

Jessica Stern of Harvard's John F. Kennedy School of Government also points out several changes in the way terrorist organizations, especially al-Qaeda, may be operating following the crackdown in Afghanistan. She claims al-Qaeda is willing to make unlikely alliances with other Islamic terrorist groups such as Hezbollah in order to expand its reach. These groups may also have morphed into less hierarchical and leaderless organizations to avoid detection. The leaders inspire small cells or individuals to take action on their own initiative instead of taking orders from above. Stern also claims Islamic terrorists are forging ties with traditionally organized crime groups.[2] If these developments are true, the threat in areas with Islamic fundamentalists in Latin America could intensify.

A recent intelligence report obtained by the *Boston Globe* seems to confirm this transformation. The report indicates US efforts against al-Qaeda are hastening its evolution from a network bound by a centralized control model of dominant figures with strong jihadist pedigrees to again resemble loosely knit groups headed by talented operatives at the local level.[3] This change may step up efforts by Islamic terrorist "sleeper cells" in Latin America to seize the initiative rather than wait for guidance from above, or to even cooperate and collaborate with Hezbollah.

Ad Hoc Radical Fundamentalists Threat

Another potential concern could be ad hoc radical fundamentalists groups forming within these small pockets of Islamic followers without any particular tie to any state support or Islamic doctrine. They may operate on a global scale and claim to act for Islam. These ad hoc groups can form quickly, require no headquarters, and have no recognized leaders. Such characteristics make them more difficult to track and apprehend than members of established groups.[4] Even with all of the tools available to US authorities, detecting and finding Islamic terrorists in the United States is difficult. Imagine how much more challenging the task is in South America.

Potential ad hoc Islamic fundamentalist groups in Latin America and the Caribbean pose a particular threat because of the fluid nature of their organization, or even lack of a formal organization. These groups can come together to carry out a single operation, much like the group responsible for bombing New York's World Trade Center in 1993. US authorities have a difficult time detecting and infiltrating these groups since they exist for such a limited period of time.[5]

One example of this type of operation might be the planned hijacking of an aircraft by nine Islamic Bangladeshis in Santa Cruz, Bolivia, in late 2003. The Bangladeshis allegedly planned to attack a US target in Argentina with an aircraft. They had been in Bolivia for a year when their suspected plot was revealed to authorities by the French police attaché. It was reported that the group was planning to fly to Buenos Aires on 2 December 2003, but Aerolineas Argentina cancelled the flight at the last minute. Apparently, the French intelligence services received information that led them to believe citizens from Bangladesh might board planes in South America, hijack them, and crash them against US targets.[6]

An Islamic Terrorist and Drug Trafficker Nexus?

Even though General Hill minimizes the connection between narco-terrorists and Islamic fundamentalists in Latin America, some experts are increasingly worried about such a possibility. Harold Wankel, the assistant administrator for intelligence at the US Drug Enforcement Agency, recently expressed a concern that al-Qaeda terrorists will turn to international drug trafficking and Colombian and/or Mexican organized crime to transport funds, people, and banned weapons.[7]

Wankel's anxiety stems from his knowledge of the crime groups' infrastructure and how valuable their network might be to al-Qaeda.

> If al-Qaida comes to South America and they need to get something done in the United States that requires movement, whether it is movement of commodity or movement of people, they need not set up infrastructure, they need not set up an operation capable of doing that. They need to get x-number of dollars and go to the people who are the professionals, the people that are the best at it, and that is the Colombian and Mexican organized criminal groups that are closely aligned these days.[8]

33

He especially worries about al-Qaeda sympathizers in Latin America who could turn to the drug trafficking network as the international crackdown on Islamic terrorists' finances dries up funds. However, at this point, it is unclear whether al-Qaeda has benefited from drug trafficking or cooperation from the narco-terrorists in the region.[9]

The first empirical evidence linking al-Qaeda with the drug trade was discovered in 2003 in the Middle East, according to a RAND terrorism expert. The US Navy seized a boat carrying nearly two tons of hashish in the Persian Gulf along with three men believed to have al-Qaeda connections. The drugs were worth between $8 and $10 million. Due to the huge profit margins involved in the drug trade, trafficking in drugs is probably becoming an attractive opportunity for al-Qaeda to rebuild its finances.[10]

Even though the principal Islamic terrorist threat in Latin America appears more related to support activities than to attacking targets in the region, are there potential areas that could be vulnerable to a strike?

Potential Islamic Terrorist Target

The purpose of this paper is not to identify every potential target for Islamic terrorists, but only to provide an example to stimulate thinking on the subject. Fortunately, there is not a significant number of potential US targets in the region except embassies and multinational businesses. Other than potential diplomatic targets like embassies and consulates, are there additional vulnerabilities and weak spots in Latin America that are ripe for an attack by Islamic terrorists? One example may stem from the United States' dependence on the region's energy exports.

Western dependence on imported petroleum and natural gas is no great secret. Nor is it a great surprise that Islamic terrorists may target energy production and the transportation supply chain. If there are any doubts about vulnerability, the bombing of the French-flagged supertanker *Limburg* off the coast of Yemen in October 2002 serves as an example. The United States' dependence on oil imports will grow from more than 50 percent today to more than 60 percent by 2010.[11] Given that rising dependence on oil and natural gas resources, an attack on these imports could bring significant economic disruption.

Today the United States imports a significant amount of petroleum from Latin America. Of the top 15 countries that export crude oil to the United States, seven are located in the Western hemisphere, including Canada. Venezuela has at times exported more oil to the United States than has Saudi Arabia, and Mexican exports are not far behind.[12]

The small island nation of Trinidad and Tobago is the number one exporter of liquefied natural gas (LNG) to the United States.[13] Its exports have grown from zero in 1998 to almost three-quarters of the imported LNG supply, mainly to terminals along the US eastern seaboard. Most of the deliveries are from supertankers carrying millions of gallons of super-chilled LNG. They dock at the terminals to unload their cargo, which is then converted to the vaporous form of natural gas for consumer use. For a creative terrorist, these transfer points could be a potential magnet for a debilitating strike.

Hitting a target like an LNG transfer point could be accomplished by any group of terrorists, Islamic or otherwise. Due to the minimal Wahabbi-Sunni fundamentalist presence in the region, an al-Qaeda hit may be unlikely. Nevertheless, one cannot completely discount the possible role of Hezbollah Shiites, ad hoc Islamic fundamentalist groups, or possible connections between Wahhabis, Hezbollah, and/or drug traffickers.

Notes

1. Jessica Stern, "The Protean Enemy," *Foreign Affairs*, July/August 2003, 19 February 2004, http://www.foreignaffairs.org/20030701faessay15403/jessica-stern/the-protean-enemy.html.

2. Ibid.

3. Bryan Bender, "Local groups giving Qaeda strength, analysis finds," *Boston Globe*, 21 November 2003, A42.

4. Jessica Stern, *The Ultimate Terrorists* (Cambridge: Harvard University Press, 1999), 6–7.

5. Ibid., 82–86.

6. Alvaro Zuazo, "Bolivia probing 9 in hijack threat," *Boston Globe*, 6 December 2003, A6.

7. Jenny Falcon, "US Official: Al-Qaeda, Drug Traffickers May Establish Ties," *Voice of America*, 2 March 2004, http://www.voanews.com/article. cfm?objectID=BD81DAD9-32C8-41EE-AAC3FBF774EEE.

8. Ibid.

9. Ibid.

10. Matt Kelley, "Qaeda link to drugs hinted," *Boston Globe*, 19 December 2003, A6.

11. Tamara Makarenko, "Terrorist threat to energy infrastructure increases," *Jane's Intelligence Review*, 1 June 2003.

12. US Department of Energy, Energy Information Administration, "Crude Oil and Total Petroleum Imports Top 15 Countries," 24 February 2004, http://www.eia.doe.gov/pub/oil_gas/petroleum/data.

13. US Department of Energy, Energy Information Administration, "Natural Gas Imports and Exports," 24 February 2004, http://www.eia.doe.gov/pub/oil_gas/petroleum/data.

Chapter 5

Policy Considerations and Conclusions

One can certainly find potential vulnerabilities other than LPG transfer sites, but fortunately Latin America is not a "target-rich" environment. A larger concern may be differences in the way the United States and Latin America perceive the primary security threats facing the region.

Prior to making effective policy recommendations, the wide gulf separating these perceptions must be addressed. These differences are especially challenging considering the cultural differences between the United States and Latin America and their long history of troubled relations.

Perceptions of the Primary Threat Facing the Region

The cultural differences and distinct concerns of the United States and Latin America can at times cause friction. For any recommended solutions to have a chance at success, both sides must address these differences and reach consensus. This divide was inadvertently highlighted by Secretary of State Colin Powell at the annual assembly of the Organization of American States in Chile on 9 June 2003. While most representatives of the 33 other nations emphasized the need for social justice, warning that democracy itself could be threatened by mounting economic difficulties and inequality, Mr. Powell was nearly alone in focusing on the triple scourge he described as "tyrants, traffickers, and terrorists."[1]

By at least recognizing and perhaps even narrowing this gap in the perception of the primary threat facing Latin America, US diplomats and military leaders may facilitate areas such as enhancing regional engagement and cooperation, strengthening monitoring efforts, and seeking to eliminate or minimize the criminal support activities.

Regional Engagement and Cooperation

There are examples of successful engagement in the region that can be expanded or used as models for other forums. One of the best models of cooperation and collaboration is the Organization of American States' Inter-American Committee Against Terrorism (CICTE). A similar, but slightly more focused example of teamwork between the United States and the countries bordering the TBA is the "Three+One" initiative. Finally, a regional roundtable made up of 19 Latin American states, called the Rio Group, is developing initiatives to improve security and minimize threats.

The CICTE forum was conceived in the mid-1990s after the two bombings in Buenos Aires. Following 9/11, CICTE took on a new sense of urgency and the frequency of the meetings has increased dramatically. The mission of CICTE is straightforward: coordinate efforts to protect the citizens of the member nations from the scourges of terrorism through the exchange of information between subject matter experts and decision makers to strengthen hemispheric solidarity and security.[2]

According to Ambassador Cofer Black, US State Department coordinator of counterterrorism, CICTE has established itself as one of the foremost regional antiterrorism bodies in the world and is recognized by the UN as a model to emulate. CICTE has developed an ambitious program focused on strengthening border and financial controls and developing sound counterterrorism legal regimes.[3] At their January 2004 session in Montevideo, delegates recognized the need to strengthen CICTE and approved a work plan to deal with aviation, port, and cyber security.[4]

The Tripartite Commission of the Triple Frontier was established in 1998 as a security mechanism by the TBA countries. When the United States joins these meetings, as it did in December 2003 in Asuncion, it becomes the "3+1" group. Three+One serves as a continuing forum for counterterrorism cooperation and prevention among all four countries. In a recent meeting, the parties discussed preventive actions against terrorism such as strengthening financial institutions, enacting money-laundering legislation, and reducing drug and arms trafficking, as well as cooperation on the exchange of information and law enforcement.[5]

The US ambassador to Brazil, Donna Hrinak, recently highlighted the growing effectiveness of security collaboration in the TBA. "Contrary to what you're hearing in the Press, the Brazilians are closely watching the TBA and cooperating with the United States. We are pleased with their level of support and the progress on clamping down on the illicit activities in the TBA."[6]

Although more liberal and less specific in nature, the Rio Group is striving to tackle some of the same issues as CICTE and "3+1" forums. Rio Group's primary concerns are threats to democratic governance, to the stability of its institutions, and to social peace. These 19 Latin American countries support a multilateral system for peace and security and view all terrorism as a threat to these goals.[7]

Improve Rule of Law and Eradicate Criminal Activities

One of the struggles in Latin America is democratic governance and adherence to the rule of law. Although progress is being made in cooperation and collaboration through the forums noted above, the challenge comes is implementing and executing the policies at the worker level. Simply because security policies and procedures are agreed upon at the international level does not mean the plan will be lawfully executed. For example, existing laws prohibit the illicit dealings in the TBA and Margarita Island, but these profitable criminal activities continue.

The concern of this study is Islamic terrorists, but whether profits are used to support terrorism or purely for greed by the mafia groups, the solution is the same: seek to eradicate the lawlessness in those regions where it flourishes. This is where improving the rule of law with regional cooperation is critical.

The challenge is outlined in a definitive Library of Congress study on terrorists and organized crime groups in the TBA. First, widespread corruption at all levels of government and law enforcement is facilitating the activities of Islamic terrorist groups and organized crime. Second, the capabilities of current security and investigative forces are inadequate for ridding the region of this problem. And finally, the laws for combating terrorist fundraising, money laundering, organized crime activities, and official corruption are also inadequate.[8]

The strained relations between the US government and some Latin American countries are increasing the challenge. However, CICTE and the "3+1" are excellent examples of working together to combat terrorism and the criminal activities that support it. The stepped-up efforts by the governments of Argentina, Brazil, and Paraguay to fight illicit activities by organized crime and terrorist groups in the TBA seem to have helped reduce these behaviors, but by no means eliminated them. US attempts to deal with Venezuela and President Hugo Chavez regarding the activities on Margarita Island may have to wait until relations improve.

Conclusions

Who will prevail in the battle for the heart of Islam, the moderates or the fundamentalists? The confrontationalists posit the clash could be a long-term struggle with repercussions not only for the United States, but also for regions like Latin America, where pockets of Islamic followers exist. If accomodationists like Esposito are correct, addressing and solving the causes of the conflict will help minimize, if not eliminate, Islamic terrorism. In either case, the implications for how the US security establishment addresses Islamic terrorism and terrorist support in Latin America and the Caribbean are profound.

If the Wahabbi-fueled fundamentalism grows and gains a stronger foothold throughout the Islamic world, research suggests the minimal threat in Latin America could increase. On the other hand, the vast majority of Muslims may repudiate the Islamic radicals and fundamentalists and embrace moderation and democracy, so the Islamic threat in the region could eventually evaporate.

CENTCOM commander Gen John Abizaid says it is going to be a long-term battle. "I think this battle of moderation versus extremism in this part of the world in particular is one that will continue well beyond the point where I'm retired," notes Abizaid.[9] Security policy makers do not have the luxury of waiting a generation for results, but must act now by answering the hard questions and developing policy accordingly.

There are two broad and strategic questions about Islamic fundamentalist terrorism in Latin America. First, despite the lack of a strong demographic or cultural connection with Lebanese and Syrian Muslim immigrants in the region, will al-Qaeda seek to develop a foothold in Latin America to sustain or expand its operations? Second, will Shiite groups such as Hezbollah continue the low profile they have maintained over the last 10 years, using the region for support activities but not direct attacks, or will they join forces with Wahabbi-oriented Sunni fundamentalists in a clash against the West?

Research suggests the following answers. First, the Islamic threat from al-Qaeda will probably not gain traction in Latin America due to the less-than-fertile ground for that form of Islamic fundamentalism. Not only are there very low percentages of all types of Muslims in the region, but the majority are Shiite Muslims, not "Wahhabi-fueled" fundamentalist Sunni Muslims. Second, Shiite fundamentalist groups like Hezbollah may strive to continue using lawless areas like the TBA and other smaller pockets in the region, but extra surveillance and increased attention by the United States in cooperation with Latin American partners will help control the problem.

Notes

1. Boris Saavedra, "Confronting Terrorism in Latin America: Latin America and United States Policy Implications," *Journal of the Center for Hemispheric Defense Studies*, National Defense University, April 2003, 220.

2. Organization of American States, Inter-American Committee Against Terrorism, 5 March 2004, http://www.cicte.oas.

3. US Department of State, Foreign Press Center briefing, "Counter-terrorism Efforts in the Organization of American States," with Ambassador Cofer Black and Ambassador John Maisto, Washington, DC, 23 January 2004, http://www.fpc.state.gov/28457.htm.

4. Draft Work Plan of CICTE and the Montevideo Declaration, *Summit of the Americas Information Network*, 4 February 2004, http://www.summit-americas.org/Quebec-hem-security.htm.

5. US Department of State news release, "Meeting of the '3+1' Counter-terrorism Group—Communiqué," 3 December 2003, http://www.state.gov/s/crls/other/2003/27057.htm.

6. Donna Hrinak, author's notes from question and answer forum at Harvard University's David Rockefeller Center for Latin American Studies, 9 March 2004.

7. Andean Community, General Secretariat, "The Cusco Consensus," May 2003, http://www.comunidadandina.org/.

8. Rex Hudson, "Terrorist and Organized Crime Groups in the Tri-Border Area (TBA) of South America," The Library of Congress, Federal Research Division, July 2003, 69–70.

9. Robert Burns, "Key general sees needs beyond Iraq," *Boston Globe,* 9 March 2004, A9.

Bibliography

Ajami, Fouad. "The Falseness of Anti-Americanism." *Foreign Policy*, September/October 2003. http://www.travelbrochure graphics.com/extra/the_falseness_of_antiamericanism.htm.

Akbarzadeh, Shahram, and Abdullah Saeed. *Islam and Political Legitimacy*. New York, RoutledgeCurzon, 2003.

Ali, Tariq. *The Clash of Fundamentalisms, Crusades, Jihads, and Modernity*. London, Verso, 2002.

Andean Community, General Secretariat. "The Cusco Consensus." May 2003. http://www.comunidadandina.org/ingles/document/GrupoRioXVII.htm.

Armstrong, Karen. "Resisting Modernity, The Backlash Against Secularism." *Harvard University Review* 25, no. 4 (Winter 2004): 40–45.

_____. "The True, Peaceful Face of Islam." *Time*, 1 October 2001. http://www.islamfortoday.com/armstrong01.htm.

Arnove, Anthony. "Islam's Divided Cresent." *The Nation*, 20 June 2002. http://www.thenation.com/doc.mhtml?I=20020708&s=arnove.

Azzam, Maha. "Al-Qaeda: the misunderstood Wahhabi connection and the ideology of violence," briefing paper no. 1, Royal Institute of International Affairs, February 2003.

Ballivan, N. "Country Perspectives, Latin America, The Spanish Ummah of the Muslim World." http://www.islamicpaths.org/Home/English/Countries/Latin_America/Spanish.

Barsamian, David. "Edward W. Said," *The Progressive*, November 2001. http://www.progressive.org/0901/intv1101.html.

Barsamian, David and Edward W. Said, "Culture and Resistance, Conversations with Edward W. Said." Cambridge: South End Press, 2003.

Boston Globe, 21 November 2003–9 March 2004.

Bryan, Anthony T., and Stephen E. Flynn. "Terrorism, Porous Borders, and Homeland Security: The Case of U.S.-Caribbean Cooperation," *North-South Update*, University of Miami, 22 October 2001. http://wwwmiami.edu/nsc/pages/newsupdates/Update49.html.

Byman, Daniel. "Should Hezbollah Be Next?" *Foreign Affairs*, November/December 2003.

Caner, Ergun M, and Emir F. Caner. "Unveiling Islam." Grand Rapids: Kregel Publications, 2002.

Carafano, James J., and Stephen Johnson. "Strengthening America's Southern Flank Requires a Better Effort." *The Heritage Foundation Policy Research & Analysis*, 20 February 2004. http://www.heritage.org/Research/National Security/bg1727.cfm.

Central Intelligence Agency. *The World Factbook*, 2003.

Chickrie, Raymond. "Muslims in Guyana. " *Muslims in Guyana: History, Traditions, Conflict and Change,* December 1999. http://www.geocities.com/WestHollywood/Park/6443/ Guyana/Guyanese_muslim.html.

Coleman, David. "Venezuelan Gatwick terror suspect was an Isla de Margarita resident." *VHeadline.com*, 16 February 2003. http://www.vheadline.com/readnews.Asp?id=3083, 25 February 2004.

Doran, Michael Scott. "The Saudi Paradox," *Foreign Affairs*, January/February 2004.

Draft Work Plan of CICTE and the Montevideo Declaration. *Summit of the Americas Information Network,* 4 February 2004. http://www.summit-americas.org/Quebec-hem-security.htm.

Elliot, Robert, and Gilbert Le Grass. "Buenos Aires Gets Biggest Mosque in Latin America." *Daily News Yahoo.com.* http:// dailynews.yahoo.com/h/nm/20000925/wl/argentina_ mosque_dc_1.html.

Encyclopedia Wikipedia, 2003 ed., "Carlos Saul Menem." http://en.wikipedia.org/wiki/Carlos_Saul_Menem.

_____. "Israeli Embassy Attack in Buenos Aires." http:// en.wikipedia.org/wiki/Israeli_Embassy_Attack_in_Buenos_ Aires.

Esposito, John L., and Francois Burgat. *Modernizing Islam.* London: Hurst & Company, 2003.

Esposito, John L. *The Islamic Threat, Myth or Reality?* Third Edition. New York: Oxford University Press, 1999.

Falcon, Jenny. "US Official: Al-Qaeda, Drug Traffickers May Establish Ties." *Voice of America*, 2 March 2004. http://

www.voanews.com/article.cfm?objectID=BD81DAD9-32C8-41EE-C3FBF774EEE.

Fox, Jonathan. "Two Civilizations and Ethnic Conflict: Islam and the West." *Journal of Peace Research*, vol. 38, no. 4, 2001, 459–72.

Fuller, Graham E. *The Future of Political Islam*, New York: Palgrave MacMillan, 2003.

Hadar, Leon T. "Covering the New World Disorder." *Columbia Journalism Review*, July/August 1994.

_____. "The 'Green Peril': Creating the Islamic Fundamentalist Threat," *Policy Analysis*, CATO Institute, August 1992.

Huntington, Samuel P. *The Clash of Civilizations and the Remaking of World Order*, first edition, New York: Simon and Schuster, 1997.

"Islam in Latin America: Lack of Islamic Literature in Brazil." *Latin American Muslim Unity*, 21 May 2001. http://www.latinmuslims.com/history/brazil_2000.html.

Johnson, Stephen. "U.S. Coalition Against Terrorism Should Include Latin America." *The Heritage Foundation Backgrounder*, no. 1489, 9 October 2001.

Juergensmeyer, Mark. "Holy Orders, Religious Opposition to Modern States." *Harvard University Review*, vol. XXV, no. 4, Winter 2004.

Kramer, Martin. "The Moral Logic of Hizballah," *Origins of Terrorism: Psychologies, Ideologies, Theologies, States of Mind*, ed. Walter Reich, Cambridge: Cambridge University Press, 1990.

_____. "Coming to Terms: Fundamentalists or Islamists?" *The Middle East Quarterly*, vol. X, no. 2, Spring 2003. http://www.meforum.org/article/541.

Lester, Toby. "What is the Koran?" *The Atlantic Online*. January 1999. http://www.theatlantic.com/issues/99jan/koran.htm.

Lewis, Bernard. *The Assassins, A Radical Sect in Islam.* New York: Basic Books, Inc, 2003.

———. *The Crisis of Islam.* New York: Random House, 2003.

Library of Congress, Federal Research Division. "The Sociology and Psychology of Terrorism: Who Becomes a Terrorist and Why?" September 1999.

Library of Congress, Federal Research Division. "Terrorist and Organized Crime Groups in the Tri-Border Area (TBA) of South America," July 2003.

Lindeborg, Lisbeth. "Osama's Library." *World Press Review Online.* 6 February 2004. http://www.worldpress.org/europe/0102dagens.htm.

Makarenko, Tamara. "Terrorist threat to energy infrastructure increases." *Jane's Intelligence Review,* 1 June 2003.

Makdisi, Ussama, "Anti-Americanism in the Arab World: An Interpretation of a Brief History." *The Journal of American History,* vol. 89, issue 2, September 2002. http://www.historycooperative.org /journals/jah/89.2/makdisi.html.

Malek, Mohammed Abdul. "A Knowledge of Arabic and Its Importance." *A Study of the Qur'an, Universal Guidance for Mankind,* January 2000. http://members.aol.com/Mamalek2/qbook2.htm.

Mendel, William W. "Paraguay's Ciudad del Este and the New Centers of Gravity." *Military Review.* Fort Leavenworth, KS, March–April 2002.

Moussalli, Ahmad S. "The Islamic Quest for Democracy, Pluralism, and Human Rights." Gainesville, FL: University of Florida Press, 2001.

Munson, Henry. "Lifting the Veil, Understanding the Roots of Islamic Militancy." *Harvard University Review,* vol. XXV, no. 4, Winter 2004.

"Muslim Situation in the Caribbean." *Muslim World League Journal.* http://www.geocities.com/WestHollywood/Park/6443/Guyana/caribbean.html.

Norris, Pippa and Ronald Inglehart. "Islam & the West: Testing the 'Clash of Civilizations' Thesis." John F. Kennedy School of Government research paper, Harvard University, Cambridge, MA, May 2002.

Oliver, Haneef James. "What is a Salafi and What is Salafism?" *The Wahhabi Myth,* May 2003. http://thewahhabimyth.com.

Organization of American States, Inter-American Committee Against Terrorism web site, 2002. http://www.cicte.oas.org/mission.htm.

Osava, Mario. "LATAM-US: Xenophobic Threats Target Arabs Everywhere." *World News*, Inter Press Service, 14 September 2001. http://www.oneworld.org/ips2/sept01/02_36_009. html.

Pape, Robert. "Dying to Kill Us." *New York Times*, 22 September 2003.

"Patterns of Global Terrorism-2001, Latin American Overview," US Department of State, Office of the Coordinator for Counterterrorism. http://www.state.gov/s/ct/pgtrpt/2001.html.

Peterson, Scott, "Foot Soldiers Propelled by Dreams of Conquering 'Infidels,'" *Christian Science Monitor.Com*, 18 October 2001. http://www.csmonitor.com/2001/1018/p14s1-wosc. htm.

Pipes, Daniel. *Miniatures, Views of Islamic and Middle Eastern Politics.* London: Transaction Publishers, 2004.

_____. *In the Path of God, Islam and Political Power.* New York: Basic Books, Inc., 1983.

Pipes, Daniel, and Graham Fuller. "Combating the Ideology of Radical Islam." http://www.anglicanmedia.com.au.news. archives/000961.php.

Potter, Angela. "Muslims That Lead Failed Coup Fined," Associated Press, 16 January 2000. http://www.hvk.org/articles/0101/86.html.

Pratt, Timothy. "US Eyes Jungle as Terror Threat Grows." *Sunday Herald Online*. http://www.sundayherald.com/ 30415.

Public Broadcasting Service. "Transcript: Bill Moyers Interviews Karen Armstrong." http://www.pbs.org/now/transcipt_armstrong.html.

Radu, Michael. "Radical Islam and Suicide Bombers." *Foreign Policy Research Institute*, 21 October 2003. http://crisis. wakeful.net/2003/Radu_suicide_bombers.html.

Robinson, Linda. "Terror Close to Home." *U.S. News & World Report*, vol. 135, no. 11 (6 October 2003): 20.

Rohter, Larry. "Bomb Case Witness: Iran Paid Off Menem." *New York Times Service.* http://www.ourjerusalem.com/ history/story/history20020724.html, 22 July 2002.

Saavedra, Boris. "Confronting Terrorism in Latin America: Latin America and United States Policy Implications." *Center for*

Hemispheric Defense Studies, National Defense University, April 2003.

Seawright, Jason. "The Official Perspective on Venezuelan Democracy," remarks at Center for Latin American Studies, UC-Berkeley, 30 October 2003. http://www.socrates. berkeley.edu/7001/Events/fall2003/10-30-03-alvarezher rera.index.html.

Schwartz, Stephen. "Communists and Islamic Extremists-Then and Now." *FrontPage magazine.com*, 8 July 2002. http://www.frontpagemag.com/Articles/ReadArticles. asp?ID=1731.

————. "Wahhabi Fireworks." *FrontPage magazine.com*, 14 July 2003. http://www.frontpagemag.com/Articles/ ReadArticles.asp?ID=8885.

————. "Daniel Pipes' Plea for Tolerant Islam," *FrontPage magazine.com*, 28 November 2003. http://www.frontpage mag.com/Articles/ReadArticles.asp?ID=10999.

————. "Islamists Invade Iraq," *FrontPage magazine.com*, 26 January 2004. http://www.frontpagemag.com/Articles/ ReadArticles.asp?ID=11900.

————. *The Two Faces of Islam, The house of Sa'ud from Tradition to Terror.* New York: Doubleday, 2002.

————. "Defeating Wahabbism." *FrontPage Magazine.com*, October 2002. http://www.frontpagemag.com/Articles/ ReadArticle.asp?ID=4178.

Skidmore, Thomas E., and Peter H. Smith. *Modern Latin America.* New York: Oxford University Press, 2001.

Stern, Jessica. *The Ultimate Terrorists.* Cambridge, MA: Harvard University Press, 1999.

————. "The Protean Enemy." *Foreign Affairs*, July/August 2003. http://www.foreignaffairs.org/20030701faessay 15403/jessica-stern/the-protean-enemy.html.

————. *Terror in the Name of God, Why Religious Militants Kill.* New York: HarperCollins, 2003.

"Terrorist Bombings in Argentina," *Jewish Virtual Library*, 2003 ed. http://www.us-israel.org/jsource/Terrorism/argentina. html.

Tinaz, Nuri. "Globalization and the Influence of Black Religio-nationalist Movement in Black Diaspora: The Case of Nation of Islam in Britain." University of Warwick, Department of Sociology, Coventry, 16 December 2003. http://www.cesnur.org/2001/london2001/tinaz.htm.

United States Congress. House Committee on International Relations Subcommittee on Western Hemisphere, Western Hemisphere Policy Statement of Dr. Robert A. Pastor, Vice President of International Affairs, 21 October 2003.

United States Department of Energy, Energy Information Administration. "Crude Oil and Total Petroleum Imports Top 15 Countries," 24 February 2004. http://www.eia.doe.gov/pub/oil_gas/petroleum/data.

————. "Natural Gas Imports and Exports," 24 February 2004. http://www.eia.doe.gov/pub/oil_gas/petroleum/data.

United States Department of State, Foreign Press Center Briefing. "Counterterrorism Efforts in the Organization of American States," with Ambassador Cofer Black and Ambassador John Maisto, Washington, DC, 23 January 2004.

United States Department of State, International Information Programs. "Report finds Gaps in U.S. Efforts Against Terror Financing," 12 December 2003. http://usinfo.state.gov/topical/econ/mlc/03121211/htm.

United States Department of State press release. "Meeting of the '3+1' Counterterrorism Group—Communiqué." http://www.state.gov/s/ct/rls/other/2003/27057.htm.

United States General Accounting Office. "Terrorist Financing, US Agencies Should Systematically Assess Terrorists' Use of Alternative Financing Mechanisms." November 2003.

Viorst, Milton. *In the Shadow of the Prophet, The Struggle for the Soul of Islam.* New York: Anchor Books, Doubleday, 1998.

Wilkinson, Paul. "The Strategic Implications of Terrorism." *Terrorism & Political Violence. A Sourcebook,* edited by Professor M.L. Sondhi, Indian Council of Social Science Research, India: Har-anand Publications, 2000.

Wilson, Scott. "U.S. probes Arabs on Venezuelan isle." *Washington Post,* 23 April 2002. A25.

Yildiz, Nurcin. "Political Islam in America Prior to Sept. 11." *Financial Times Information.* 8 November 2003.

Zacharias, Ravi. "Light in the Shadow of Jihad." Sisters, Oregon: Multnomah Publishers, Inc., 2002.

Understanding Islam and Its Impact on Latin America

Air University Press Team

Chief Editor
Jerry L. Gantt

Copy Editor
Lula Barnes

Book Design and Cover Art
Daniel M. Armstrong

*Composition and
Prepress Production*
Mary P. Ferguson

Print Preparation
Joan Hickey

Distribution
Diane Clark

www.ingramcontent.com/pod-product-compliance
Lightning Source LLC
Chambersburg PA
CBHW082151290526

45794CB00008B/3245